DEVELOPING
PLANETARY
ETHICS

DEVELOPING PLANETARY ETHICS

The Urgent Work of Today's Generation

Terry P. Anderson
Sandra Maslow Smith

Path of Potential

DEVELOPING PLANETARY ETHICS

PHOTOGRAPHY
Carol Anderson
BJ Clark
Candi Clark
Rebecca Fassler
Sandra Maslow Smith

COVER AND BOOK DESIGN
Candi Clark

GRAPHICS AND PRINTING
Candi Clark
Sunburst Graphics & Printing, Inc.
Grand Junction, CO 81503 USA

STYLISTIC EDITOR
Paige Gengenbach

PUBLISHER
Path of Potential
P.O. Box 4058
Grand Junction, CO 81502 USA
www.pathofpotential.org

AUTHORS
Terry P. Anderson
Sandra Maslow Smith

First Printing - 2007
Printed in the United States of America
30% Post Consumer Waste Fiber,
Acid Free, Archival Quality

ISBN-10: 0-9760139-4-0
ISBN-13: 978-0-9760139-4-5

CONTENTS

*"Today's generation," in one way, refers to those
to whom the future belongs,
but it also includes all those upon whom the future depends –
those who willfully join in
the urgent work of developing planetary ethics.*

The Urgent Work

Developing planetary ethics is the reflective work... the "called for" work... the grassroots work... of today's generation. In order to develop planetary ethics we need to develop and have a living philosophy. In developing a living philosophy, we must be conscious of and choiceful about the perspective we hold, for our perspective ultimately determines the life path we take and our thinking and behavior along that path - the way we live and work. Wholeness, and imaging the virtuous working of the whole, is the new starting point for developing the planetary ethics essential for filling today's ethical void.

How to Read this Book

The intended purpose and work of "Developing Planetary Ethics" is to evoke dialogue... the nature of reflective dialogue essential for communities to develop their own living philosophy. A living philosophy is a philosophy sufficiently encompassing and whole to enable people of all walks of life – people who have at heart the renewal of humanity and the healthy working of earth – to come together to create the planetary ethics we so urgently need at this time.

It is the hope that "Developing Planetary Ethics" will not only lift up for us the necessary work of today's generation, but also provide the nature of orientation needed to take on this work as well as reflective examples of its doability.

Written in the language of intuition, this collection of personal reflections contains neither conclusions nor opinions commonly gained by analysis of facts and data, but rather images of truth that both seek and lend themselves to further deepening and increasing wholeness. Here, one is reading to gain an image of the working of the whole, an image meant to become a source for further reflection and dialogue. So first read this book from cover to cover, letting the images generated enter your heart. Secondly, in a series of grassroots gatherings, read each paper aloud. Follow the reading with reflective dialogue. End each gathering by sharing images, actions and work that can be put into practice within your community... always remembering, if love is not present in the process, love will not be present in the outcome.

*If love is not in the process,
it will not be in the outcome.*

*Demonizing, attacking, defending and justifying are
not the ways of love, of intuition, of wholeness...
they are not ways leading to the planetary ethics
we now need.*

*With love flowing into and through our hearts,
the ethics we create will be whole...
they will be planetary...
and they will be sourced in virtue.*

*If love is not present in the process,
love will not be present in the outcome.*

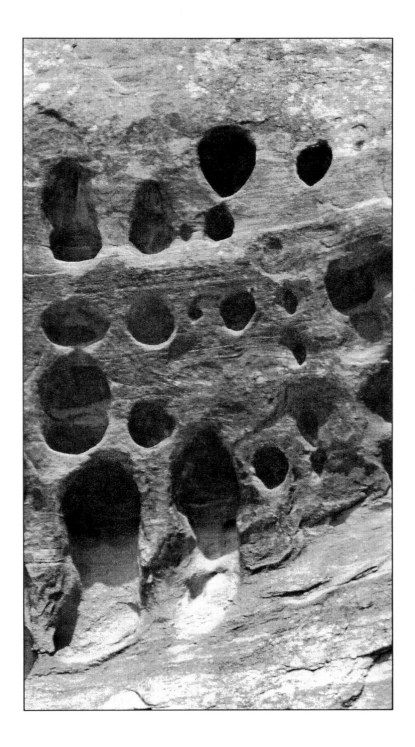

Part I

Philosophy and Ethics
Developing Ethics is the
Work of Philosophy

11

THE LIVING PHILOSOPHY OF POTENTIAL

Our work through the years has been shaped, formed and guided towards the pursuit of philosophy – more specifically a practical, practice-able, living philosophy of potential... not something to be treated as a separate subject of human knowing, but rather an orderly and wholistic thought system that – given the realities of today's world and the challenges facing humankind and life itself – could be meaningfully understood and applied in daily living... and lived out in harmony with one's faith. This has been for us, in one way or another, a lifetime pursuit... a pursuit that has been one of wandering along a path that at times has seemed to be rather tortuous. This path, however (some sixty plus years later), is beginning to come into fruition and reasonably useful coalescence, not to an endpoint (as we have come to understand the pursuit of truth is an unending one), but hopefully a useful basis for practice and development.

We looked out into the world in which we live, and macroscopically could see that "we the people" were in a bit of a free fall... a free fall in the sense of not living a life we believe in. If we look about through reflective receptivity versus analysis and angst, we notice several things repeatedly happening. We see most thinking is starting from economics, legality and rights. These perspectives, particularly in the manner in which they are being held, are commonly sources of divisiveness; they are not realistic means for lifting us up to become more fully and truly human, nor do these perspectives provide the solving power for the significant issues and challenges facing humanity, earth and life itself. In addition, we can see ongoing conflicts which, in the current way of behaving, seem irreconcilable – conflicts between religions, between religion and science, between and within political processes and parties, etc. And so we haveconcluded that the real void is philosophy: Without a contribution from philosophy we will not be able to progress in our humanness, not be able to bring about reconciliation (versus compromise) -true upward progression - opposite the planetary challenges facing humanity and life itself.

This philosophical void has become more apparent as we have talked with people about the subject of ethics, the generation of ethics of course being the work and output of philosophy. When the term first comes up, people often say, "You mean morality, don't you?" ...to which we reply, "No, ethics... the behavioral principles we as a society establish and impose upon our selves and each other – particularly on those in critical roles in essential systems (e.g. government, education, religion, press, etc.)." With that little bit of reminding, people quickly grasp the notion and rapidly recognize the void – seeing the absence of ethics in essentially all of our social processes, systems and institutions. They share the notion that "being legal" has replaced the ideal of "being ethical," of living above the law (for example, driving so that other drivers are safer rather than merely driving within the legal limits).

And so, if the critical work of today's generation - those who are spirited and "young at heart" - is to create the processes for us to become ethical, then we must go about the work of developing a philosophy that has sufficient completeness, depth of scope, and wholeness to be a real source of the planetary ethics required... a philosophy that embraces the essential human characteristic of our yearning to become... a philosophy that will both strengthen faith, and be strengthened by faith. Faith tied to weak philosophy runs the risk of becoming a myth or superstition... and philosophy that is not strengthened by faith turns away from our "beingness." These weaknesses have brought us to the common experience of today, an experience of reason anchoring itself to the physical, and material being seen as the only legitimate, provable real aspect of our existence.

In our work, we have come to the living philosophy of potential. At the heart of this living philosophy is the work of leading from virtue, that is essence, and as such, requires that we call upon intuition – the nature of intuition required for seeing the whole of something and its right and good working. This philosophy, as is common among philosophies, deals with the meaning of life and existence, but is unique in that it looks at existence from the perspective of essence (versus from the perspective of material/physical)... and significantly, we have come to understand essence as being the pattern of intention of the Creator. We have also come to understand that planetary ethics, if they are to be truly planetary, require we as a people shift from being human centered to being life of the whole centered - the whole of humanity, the whole of life - a perspective that acknowledges the truth of our design: We are living beings, members in the community of life.

Understanding the Work and Working of Ethics

In one sort of way, we could describe ethics as the behavioral guidelines (principles and rules) which we willfully impose upon ourselves, or consciously accept as real requirements of particular roles that we take on,

especially roles that involve systems or institutions that are critical to the healthy working of our society. At times we experience ethics as an inner talking preceding an action – an action which, if we listen carefully, we know in our heart of hearts as to whether or not it is a right and good (right for the one, good for the whole) thing to do… or at the very least, harmless to the whole and others. Besides the inner talking, there is the experience and process of the community speaking – at times to itself, but frequently to those in essential roles in systems and institutions critical to the well being of society (for example, education, religion, business, government, recreation, entertainment, press, and on and on). We notice this "community speaking" most often in regard to what is commonly thought of as scandalous behavior, a "speaking" that often takes the form of outrage, expectations of corrective actions (consequences) by those in charge, and increasingly legal action, especially when the community perceives inadequate or inappropriate corrective action by the "powers that be." This "community speak" seems to take its strength and its sense of obligation and responsibility from the reality that in America, power goes from the people to its institutions – not only our governing institutions, but the critical institutions of society as well. The community, recognizing the absolute necessity for having trust and confidence in the working, decision-making, and actions of these institutions, turns to ethics - the higher plane, that which is above the law - to ensure right and good management of these institutions.

Now a curious thing has been happening of late. There is a tendency to start our thinking from the perspective of legality. Thus perhaps we may automatically think "legal action" when scandalous behavior occurs. There also is a tendency to lump all "scandalous behavior" into the category of morals or morality. The effect of both of these is that ethics, ethicality and ethical behavior are in a real sort of way disappearing from our consciousness, and therefore from our conscientiousness. The ethical vigilance required to sustain the vitality, vigor and viability of our society, is relatively inactive – "off the screen" of our everyday life so to speak. Yet we know, intuitively obvious is the truth, that the destiny of an unethical society is disorder, collapse and ruin… which brings to mind this notion: The question is not so much one of "Did we come from apes?" but rather one of "Where are we going – toward apes, or towards truly human?"

To sort out the contrasting difference and work of morals and ethics is beyond the scope of this reflection, but perhaps a few comments that emerged from a recent conversation with a friend would be helpful. Stated most simply, morals are between you and your Maker. Ethics are between you, me and the community. Moral infractions carry with them the possibility of forgiveness, a forgiveness that calls for genuine sorrow and contriteness, with the ultimate judgment in the hands of your Maker. Ethical infractions, from an American perspective, carry with them the possibility of restoring the people's trust and confidence in the perpetrator and institutions, a possibility (at least for the institutions) that has to be realized if we are to sustain a healthy working society; thus exists the requirement for overtness, clarity of corrective action, and the necessity for consequences, up to and including removal from the role. We can see from a healthy working society standpoint, "moral forgiveness" in and of itself is inadequate for those which are truly "ethical infractions" - those infractions which violate the trust and confidence so necessary to sustaining our critical institutions.

The subject of this writing is planetary ethics. Here we are

being called upon to add to our experience and understanding of societal ethics, the planet and mother earth, and so the conversation has to shift. Now the "inner talking" and "community speaking" need to include the voice of earth herself... hearing and heeding her cries.

Coming to Grips with Essential Questions

The central dilemma facing today's generation is the lack of and the inability to generate ethics - ethics for the emerging world of today.

If we are serious about our desire and the necessity to change our current way of interacting among each other within our communities and places of work, between and among our societal constituencies, and between countries, and if our wish is to create ways that are more hopeful – have more rightness and goodness within them – then the work we must take on is the developing of ethics... ethics that not only serve ourselves – the whole of humanity – but the whole of life itself. In essence, these ethics must embrace living on the planet earth.

It is the work and purpose of philosophy to generate ethics. In the absence of philosophy, we become unable – disenabled – to create ethics. Whereas morality seems to fall within the domain of faith, ethics and ethical behavior emanate from philosophy. Thus, when we work to generate ethics - planetary ethics - we must begin with the development and creation of philosophy, a philosophy whole enough and complete enough to embrace the requirement of dealing with right and good living on the planet earth.

Recognizing this work and the criticality and urgency for this work, what follows here are some thoughts that hopefully, will provide a basis for reflection and dialogue among all who, with good heart and spirit, join in the work of developing the ethics – the guides to our behavior – for living in today's world on the planet earth.

When seeking to develop a living philosophy - one that is capable of being practiced in our daily life – we must come to grips with some critical questions and notions that not only determine the path we go down, but provide substantive resolution to both our hearts and minds - our conscience and our conscious intellect. For if we are seeking a philosophy that is sufficiently whole and complete to provide guidance for living on this planet earth, it is a necessity that we too can experience increasing wholeness and completeness as we work to develop the discipline – the ethical behavior – to carry out this philosophy in our daily living and working. We have to answer the following questions with heartfelt conviction – give a real YES or NO to these questions, and accept the answers we generate. Only answers true in our hearts are those which we will follow – answers that through reflection and our experience of life, ring true for us.

Is there a Source, an Ultimate Source of creation?

Is there intention in the design of the ongoing creation?

In reality, in essence and in truth, are we not one people – one people of earth - sharing a common Source, sharing a common humanity, sharing a common membership in the larger community of life?

Do we – each and all of us - have potential as human beings?

Is there within us something enfolded that is not yet manifested – a good yet to be expressed?

When we are awake to our innermost self, do we experience an urge to become... to become better... to be more REAL to ourselves and others?

Is it reasonable to expect that we can discover the truths related to wholeness and life's processes by examining separate elements or aspects?

Must our seeking turn to reflection and contemplation which work to see wholeness and the working of systemic elements within the whole?

Is it not the nature of life and the character of life's members to have purpose?

Could not the discovering and working to fulfill our purpose be a means to realize our potential and a source of ongoing meaning in our life?

Does not life purpose, which emanates from the whole of life and its working, demand that any purpose, if it is to be true to life, reflect our work and obligation to larger wholes of which we are a part?

Must the ethics that we generate describe ways of honoring the wholeness of our fellow creatures of earth, and honor their way of working and their way of becoming?

Should not the philosophy that is the source of our ethics be, at a minimum, complementary with the essence of our living faith?

Should not our philosophy provide insights into and guidance for ethical exploration and manifestation of the life, material and energy worlds of our scientific endeavors?

Does not our philosophy demand that we accept our living nature and systemic connectedness to other life members, and therefore require us to take on a responsible role in the working and ongoingness of life's processes on earth?

Does not our potential lie along the path of intention – our purpose, our essential reason for being?

Does not community have an essential role in our process of uncovering and realizing our potential?

Is not community essential to our fulfilling the intent for which we were designed?

Must we not have faith that within the scope of our design, there lies the means to create and the capacity to live and work in ways that are beyond sustaining ourselves and our lives as humankind – to live and work in ways that enable unfolding and realizing the potential of life, life's community, and life's members?

These questions are the beginning of a process to bring forth a perspective sufficiently whole and complete for the emerging world of today.

Embracing a New More Whole and Hopeful Perspective

We can, through personal reflection and a bit of dialogue with concerned fellow citizens, begin to see and identify some of our commonly held perspectives – perspectives that have become habitual starting points for our thinking... and therefore have determined our actions. Economic desires, legal action, and exercising rights are certainly among the most common of these perspectives.

With a bit more reflection and reflective dialogue we can see how these common perspectives work to blind us to, or at least make obscure, higher notions. We notice that economic desires work to obscure virtue and virtuousness; legal action – reliance on law – distracts and seduces us away from the concerted effort required to develop wholistic and genuine ethics; exercising rights not only blinds us to dignity, but also greatly inhibits our ability to come together to create real solutions – solutions not only right for the one, but right and good for all.

What emerges from our reflection and dialogue is not a condemnation of these common perspectives (economic, legal, rights), but rather a real, yet somewhat unsettling, recognition of their limitations. We become aware of their lack of wholeness: Their lack of including the whole of humanity and the whole of life. We can see the output of these perspectives as more often leading to separateness, fractionation and, if unchecked, divisiveness... hindering our coming together in a process of accessing and building the wisdom necessary to provide the guidance required for developing wholistic ethics and wholistic ways of living and working. We need ethics that not only regenerate an inner sense of goodness in the ways we are living, but provide a true sense of hope for us and our children... ethics that can bring a renewed sense of faith in our ability to generate real and lasting solutions to the multitude of major issues facing humanity – issues such as environment, peace and health.

The new perspective needs to be one that includes each and all, honoring the uniqueness of each, yet good for all... one that serves humanity, not selfishly, but wholistically... one that recognizes that ultimately our well being is directly and totally affected by the well being of earth and her planetary life-giving systems and processes. The new perspective needs to be one that acts from the truth of our design: We are living beings, as dependent upon earth's vitality - clean air, clean water, and vigorously healthy living systems (for example, estuaries) and processes (for example, pollination) - as are all of our fellow creatures of earth; and one that recognizes that we have a common Source, the Source of the ongoing creation.

As we are working on this new perspective, we hope that we the people will be able – in our heart of hearts – to say that we feel good about "how we are living" and "what we are living for," and that we will be able to consciously and in good conscience say, "We as a people are doing okay." To do so requires we be ever vigilant to see that our perspective is sufficiently whole and imbued with sufficient rightness and goodness.

Leading from Virtue and Wholeness

Leading our thinking from virtue and wholeness provides a new starting point – an authentic reference point – for generating the ethics we now need...

Such that we are truly prepared for taking on the work of addressing the significant issues of our time...

In a way that we can continue on the path of becoming more fully and truly human...

Always remembering that regardless of the cleverness of our solutions, in the absence of ethics - planetary ethics – we will not be moving along the path of intention.

Virtue and Wholeness - A New Starting Point

For years, our work has aimed at making visible a pathway towards our becoming more fully and truly human, and towards seeing ways of bringing meaningful and lasting solutions to issues such as divisiveness, development and ecology. From very early on, the necessity to call upon intuition and conscience became clear, intuition being that which we call upon to experience and "see" virtue and to image wholeness, its right and good working and the systemic relatedness of its elements; and conscience meaning we could conscientiously act from and live out truths that were made visible and heartfelt.

Both intuition and conscience require the process of reflection... reflection, not in and of itself yielding wholeness and wisdom, but rather being an initiating and awakening process for intuition. Through the processing and development of the living philosophy of potential emerged the phrase, "Giving voice to intuition and courage to conscience," a phrase that itself emerged from many people expressing their experience with words like, "Yes, now I see more clearly, more wholly, more truthfully, that which I have been intuiting."

This initial insight, "voice to intuition and courage to conscience," has not only sustained itself, but has become more deeply understood... a reality that continues to affect the nature of writings and dialogues that occur. As we read and reflect on what is written here, let us remind ourselves that just as reflection is the initiating process for awakening and accessing intuition, wholeness and imaging the virtuous working of the whole is the new starting point for developing planetary ethics... an understanding that for a growing number, is becoming intuitively obvious.

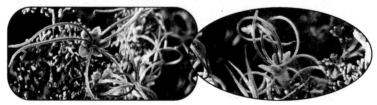

The Importance of We the People Differentiating Morality and Ethicality

The aim of this reflection is not one of producing scholarly definitions or legal tenets, but rather to create practical images and imagery of the working of morality and ethicality – two critical, distinctive, but complementary processes of any healthy working community or society. The emphasis on practical (that is, being able to be practiced or carried out) comes from the belief and recognition that ultimately the decisions and behaviors of our daily living and working determine the depth and nature of morality and ethicality of a society. The people – the people's way of living and way of working - are the final determinant. The foundational phrase, the cornerstone of our country, "we the people," is what is required to be called upon and made operational, acknowledging the responsibility and accountability that lies within we the people, ourselves. Thus it falls upon us to develop the capacity for understanding and managing morality and ethicality. The ability to effectively deal with the realms of virtue and vice, and right and good societal system behavior is critical – both in terms of providing a stable platform for our daily living and working, and as a means for realizing the potential that lies within and before us.

Both of these processes – morality and ethicality – deal with being and becoming. They work to provide intellectual, emotional, behavioral and spiritual guidance for what we want to be, need to be, or could become. We can see and experience the capacity of both to be an uplifting force within ourselves and our society. At the same time, we can witness the degeneration and erosion of greatness and potential within ourselves and our society as ethicality and morality become less present, less of a force in our daily living and working. Both seem to have the character of truth in that appreciation for and understanding of the processes of ethicality and morality can be deepened and broadened through reflection, contemplation, dialogue and experience. As we as a people develop and evolve our capacity to understand and live to higher ideals, so too must morality and ethicality develop and evolve. As we pursue and work to bring about higher value and more meaningful planes of existence (life platforms that allow, demand and enable us to be more fully human and to bring forth and realize our human potential), morality and ethicality must not only accompany us on the journey, but also must grow and develop accordingly. Woven into an essential aspect of the intent and design of the human are the processes of morality and ethicality. It is intended and required that we be both moral and ethical. Without these characteristics, our humanness - the truth of our humanity - disappears.

Morality seems to be innerly centered. It is an intrinsic process. Its work appears to be character building. Morality is the inner struggle and processing in which we engage to develop command over the qualities essential to the character we are trying to be and the virtues we are trying to manifest and use as a guide for living. We experience the struggle as we deal with the temptations and vices that work to distract us from our aim, from our effort to become a more virtuous, truer self. This struggle is a common and ongoing experience for each and all of us – if not in the forefront of our mind, at least in the form of a lingering echo. This struggle, this process, seems to be innate - an essential part of our design - and perhaps it is the process by which we become dignified human beings. Because it is such an intrinsic aspect of our selves, we can readily relate to and empathize with the trials, the tribulations, and the failings of our fellow humans. As such, the idea or notion of forgiveness (of ourselves and others) for non-moral actions and transgressions becomes integrated into human processes and interactions. Forgiveness recognizes the reality of failure, but neither honors nor condones the act itself. In a sense, forgiveness suspends judgment and works to relieve and dissipate negative energy – be it within one's self or towards one another.

As a community, as a society, we enter into this personal and usually private struggle when someone's behavior so affects the community that the community is unable to live from its desired moral character or moral plane. Most often, this occurs when individuals are engaging in behaviors that are anchored in the lesser aspects of ourselves. As a community, we seem to understand the necessity for encouraging and demanding behaviors that emanate from and call forth the higher aspects of ourselves, those aspects that more truly reflect our humanness, thus we give honor and esteem to those who have developed and are demonstrating the capacity to live and work from virtue. Through reflection and experience, we can see that the American commitment to elevating human dignity and realizing the open-ended potential of each and all, requires continuous development of character; there is an ongoing and critical need for us to be moral and for morality to be present and at work.

Ethicality seems to be more of an extrinsic or externally generated process. Its realm appears to be related to the systems and processes of one's community or society. In particular, it deals with societal roles and the behavioral expectations that society holds for the particular role. The focus of its effort, its work, is ensuring predictable behavior. Society recognizes that the integrity, the trustworthiness, and the sustainability of its systems, is directly dependent upon the ethics and the ethical behavior of those who fill the roles within the system - the systems being all those that have been developed to support, sustain, and advance the core processes of human life and work (for example, educating our children, maintaining our health, governing community life, producing food, clothing and shelter, etc.).

Within these systems, essential to the effective operation of these systems, are roles. Roles have both a being and doing character. They require not only a particular level of skill and knowledge, but also particular characteristics and qualities – thus a way of doing, an expected behavior. Roles commonly include accountability for resources and a responsibility for sustaining the integrity of the process.

In a real sense, society is entrusting an individual with the conscious and conscientious carrying out of a systemic role critical to the vitality and viability of society. Ethicality, then, comes forth to determine the appropriate - the right and the good - behavior of the person in the role relative to other individuals within the system, the effective working of the system, and the sustaining and advancement of the processes of the system the role is there to serve. Whereas morality seems to be concerned about ideals, ethicality seems to be more concerned with standards. Whereas forgiveness enters when one misses the mark relative to an ideal, consequences spring to life relative to non-ethical behavior. The need to enforce and experience consequences appears to be related to the depth of trust that accompanies these societal roles.

Morality - the process we engage in for character development and for the perfecting of our society and ourselves - reacts differently to offenses and failures than does ethicality. Morality seems to be a more individualized, patient, and through-time process – except when it threatens the character development of society as a whole.

Ethicality seems to have a more immediate concern or reaction; it seems to be responding to that which is threatening the health, vitality and viability of the whole. Ethicality understands the essential nature of a system where the behavior of one element (one role) affects the working and behavior of all the elements (all the roles). It understands the devastating nature of the consequences of un-checked non-ethical behavior. It clearly sees the consequences that inevitably occur to us as a people, to our children, and to humanity, as systemic role integrity degrades, and as confidence, credibility and trust disappear. It knows only too well that proliferation of non-ethical behavior ultimately destroys our capacity for accessing the most fundamental building blocks of humanity – faith, hope and compassion. For when a society – particularly the youth of a society – loses faith in its critical systems, and experiences hopelessness in and through these systems, the society loses its capacity for compassion, turns, and consumes itself. Given this understanding, it is not surprising that ethicality acts more swiftly and harshly when ethical standards of behavior are violated; removal or restriction of the individual in the role is common and deemed appropriate. The elimination of an intolerant risk is predominating. Concern for the preservation of the whole, its potential, and its possibilities, out-weighs the concern for the individual. Ethicality works to be vigilant, to guard against the all too common ego driven illusion that the ends justify the means. It continually battles the force that enters into and influences us in a way that we believe our ideas are so noble and right that any means are justifiable. It seems to recognize and understand that if love is not in our process - in our means - it will not be present in the ends we pursue. This vigilance, this commitment to sustain the integrity of critical human systems, is the true gift of ethicality.

It is intended and necessary that both of these processes – morality and ethicality – operate at a level above the laws of society. Morality and ethicality are being and becoming processes. They are what we engage in to go beyond… to be more than what we currently are, and to reflect the quality and strength of character to which we aspire. Social law or legality, by nature, does not evoke the spirit and willfulness possible through the envisionment of a more virtuous life or way of living – particularly as it relates to future generations. The work of legality seems to be more in the realm of keeping us on track, or perhaps keeping us from slipping backwards. Morality and ethicality are truly distinctive, but complementary processes. How these processes operate and how they react to transgressions is unique to each. Both are critical to the sustaining and development of our humanness and human potential. Because of their uniqueness and criticalness, it is important that we as a people can differentiate and discern issues arising in our society as to whether they are issues of morality or issues of ethicality. Confusing the two and responding inappropriately can have grave and lasting consequences. On the other hand, the right and good working of these processes produces a base from which America and all of America's people can pursue and experience elevated dignity, realize open-ended potential, and create a greater future for life as a whole and for the whole of life.

Rekindling the Process Fire of Developmental Work

Central to the living philosophy of potential is the notion of work... work that is related to the bringing forth, the unfolding, of enfolded potential. This work, even when we experience it as an individual, is always carried out in the context of a larger whole - something greater than ourselves, often a system, a living system of which we are a

part. As such our work and our purpose become, in many ways, one and the same. This work, this unfolding of enfolded potential, is the process by which we develop – develop as a person, and as a human society... the very means for being and becoming – the way of our calling, of fulfilling our purpose... our reason for being – the path toward becoming fully and truly human... the process, the very means for fulfilling the intent and design of the Creator.

As we reflect on our lives, the life process of children, of the elderly, of life itself, we can begin to see the inherent presence, character and particular purpose associated within and through the stages of life. We notice that even in the very early stages of childhood there is an intent – a clear focus of effort at a particular purpose or work. We see it as we "watch in wonder," a child struggling to roll over... the countless attempts, the determination to succeed. Our amazement only increases as we watch the child exercise this new "roll over" capacity, and quickly begin to work to extend it to crawling... each child seeming to develop their own unique way, but all sharing in a determination to gain the capacity – the ableness – to move from where they are to some other place. It is here that we often begin to see the essential nature and character of developmental work: The inclusion and requirement – the presence – of being and will. Now we see not just the doing, but the willfulness and the generation and managing of being – the overcoming of frustration, the emergence of patient determination, and the obvious joy and sharing of joy that accompanies each successful try.

Now, continuing our reflecting, we can see further unfolding. Crawling becomes a platform for developing walking capacity, walking joins with emerging talking capacity, and a personality begins to show up, all of which become a means for joining in, for developing our capacity for having a role in the family and other living systems of which we are a part. These unfoldings of the enfolded, when we appreciatively see and reflect upon them, take on the character of being miraculous – a beauty and joy beyond the factually explainable. And when this occurs we can, through our participation – our presence in the process – experience love entering into the working of the world… perhaps that is the source of the inner and outer joy, the joy of intentionality, of carrying out the intended.

Upon further reflection, we see the truth of development and developmental work not being restricted to childhood, but rather intended to be present and active throughout our lives. We notice that the work becomes increasingly inner in nature – less external, and more intrinsic. Somewhere along the way we notice that development work – when we are working developmentally – has a reciprocal character, in that as we develop the work, it develop us, and vice versa. And too we notice that in addition to the doing, being and will aspects of the work, spirit begins to enter – to be more present, more active, more accessible. Along with spirit, meaning and purpose also show up – often in the form of questions about one's own life, questions that seem to increase in relevancy as one ages, questions which, if honored, can be experienced with the nature of urge and urgency we had as a child as we strove to crawl and walk… all of which require the active presence of intentionality, not so much in a goal sort of way, but rather related to being and becoming.

Developmental work does not occur mechanically or in a vacuum. Nor, even though it is inherent within us, does it occur without enablement and effort. If we extend our childhood reflections to the teenage/young adult stage, we can begin to see this at work. At this stage of our life we are really called to make life real. The world we live in is a dynamic, evolving and often dramatic place. The world that is emerging and unfolding before the young adult is not the world that was emerging when their parents or grandparents were young adults. While wisdom is an ongoing need, there is a requirement to develop a frame of reference – a philosophy – that not only enables ongoing development, but also one that reflects the reality – the realness – of the emerging world. In some ways the developmental work of this stage of life can be considered the most critical to our future – not only as individuals, but to humanity as well... a criticality that becomes clearer as we recall that development – developmental work – is the process, the inherent process, by which we advance our humanness. If a generation does not engage in – take up – this developmental work, we risk the loss of development itself, the loss of our ability to advance our humanness. Losing the capacity to advance our humanness results not in the sustaining of our current level of humanness, but inevitably leads to a retreat, a real move towards being and becoming less and less human – a true regression, rather than progression, along our intended path.

In much the same way that the young adult is called upon to develop a frame of reference, a philosophy, that not only enables our continuous development as human beings, but reflects the emerging reality of that which is unfolding, there are times when the people – as a whole, as a living system – are called upon to take up and engage in similar work. Today is such a time... a time for reflection, a time for action, and particularly a time for wise choices. Wisdom is every bit, if not more so, as essential to the called for work of the people as it is to the young adult. The making of wise choices will be greatly benefited by an understanding of the two types of work: (1) Arresting entropy - arresting run down, and (2) negentropic - run up. While these types of work are common to living systems, the perspective of the living philosophy of potential provides a particular coloring to each.

Imaging run down (arresting entropy) work, we begin to picture some critical elements and see, if not a systemic nature, at least their relationship as a set. We see for instance that this work tends to anchor itself in existence. It acknowledges that that which comes into existence tends to run down - thus the effort to arrest run down. For example, roads need repairing, houses require maintenance, water and air need to be cleaned of pollutants, etc. Arresting run down calls upon intellect and reason, follows a problem solving path, and looks to analysis, segmentation, facts and proof.

Imaging run up work we also begin to see some of its elements and patterns. Here we, of necessity, work to see systemic relatedness, how each element systemically relates to the others, and how its work and role affects the working of all others and of the whole... a working relatedness that the statement, "If you touch one, you touch them all," helps us to keep in mind. Envisioning the whole, its right and good working and the systems and systemic relatedness within become primary. Here the anchor is essence rather than existence; potential versus problem becomes the orientation and approach; intuition - the intuition of wholeness - is called upon; and the seeking of wisdom, developing wise choices, and wisdom guiding reason come to the fore. At this time, in the dramatic reality of today, a further demand is placed upon run up work, that being the demand to shift - to shift as a people, a people of earth - from being human centered to being life of the whole centered. In the absence of a life of the whole perspective, we cannot carry out the nature of run up work required... the work that is absolutely necessary, not only for humanity, but for life itself.

A life of the whole perspective, by its very nature, both enables and seeks the seeing of the whole and the systemic relatedness within. It acknowledges the truth of our design – that we are living human beings, and therefore members in the community of life. It is a perspective that allows us to see the systemic relatedness of today's issues – issues such as environment, world peace and poverty - and to pursue systemic and wholistic solutions and pathways, thus bringing a potential for a real possibility of lasting solutions, solutions which advance our humanness. By way of contrast, if we reflect on an arrest entropy approach – an arresting run down and human centered approach – we notice we not only see ourselves as separate from – outside of - the environment, for example, but also tend to see environment as separate from world peace, and atmospheric carbon as separate from estrogenic compounds in earth's water systems. The hazard here is that what gets generated are partial solutions; each "problem" can become a separate "cause", and a source of effort, energy and resource expenditure that occurs out of the context of the whole and its right and good solutions, often resulting in partial solutions that show up elsewhere as serious problems or issues. With a tiny bit of reflection, we can call upon a wealth of experience where that which we did to fix a problem resulted in an issue or problem of equal or greater seriousness.

Now, to be clear, there has always been the presence and need for both types of work – arresting run down and run up – and there exists within each a real possibility for developmental processes and developmental work. Commonly at issue is the question of balance, and perhaps today the issue is the need for shifting the imbalance – that is, not shifting from being heavily weighted towards arresting run down to some middle point, but rather shifting to being heavily weighted in the direction of run up work. This emphasis towards run up work seems to be not only valid for activity, but also for that from which we take our direction: That which leads our thinking surely must be anchored in a life of the whole perspective, regardless of the type of work we are engaging in.

And so, as we look out at the multitude of issues facing ourselves and life itself (for example, world peace, energy security, ecology, poverty, divisiveness of culture and religion and of religion and science), what therefore is the work – the called for work - of today's generation, the work that a life of the whole perspective enables us to see, the work that truly could bring reconciling power, and would enable our continuing to advance in our humanness – to move forward along our intended path? More and more of us are seeing with increased clarity and conviction that the work of today's generation is that of developing planetary ethics... ethics that will not only bring to us hope and renewed faith in our human systems and institutions, but will also encompass the whole of life... and by so doing begin the development of a platform – a platform of advanced and advancing humanness – upon which we can live and work... and upon which all of life and life's processes can thrive.

Being Integration... Our Way of Becoming Whole

A source image, an image of what is required of us, for developing planetary ethics...

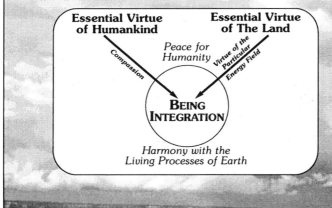

The work for which we are now being called upon is to bring about the being integration of humankind's essential virtue of compassion with the essential virtue of the land upon which we live and work… remembering the Source of both is the Creator. Holding both harmoniously and equally within our heart of hearts makes real the possibility of peace for humanity, and living in harmony with the processes of earth.

Reflecting on the image, its wholeness, seeing its right and good working, and understanding the systemic relatedness of its elements will, through inner processing and dialoguing, provide a means out of which can emerge planetary ethics, true planetary ethics – living principles that will enable our ways of living and working to be right and good for humanity, and equally right and good for earth, the whole of life, and all of its members.

Work and roles are the practical means by which these ethics become real for us… work and roles, understood and taken on, not only for ourselves, our families, and our communities, but also for the systems, processes and institutions critical for the healthy working of humanity, and for the healthy working of life itself.

Part II

Work and Roles
- Taking Issues to Essence -

This collection of personal reflections is shared with the hope that through 'seeing' the working of a living philosophy in many and various arenas, each reader will begin to build an image from which to create a living community philosophy of potential... a philosophy from which all in the community might come together to develop the planetary ethics that we and the world so urgently need at this time.

Beginning Thoughts on Repotentializing the Gulf Coast

The last time I was in to see my dental hygienist, she told me a childhood story of walking for miles along the Gulf Coast, while taking in the ever-active nourishing and replenishing processes of nature. It was pristine and it was beautiful.

Such a story has the power to evoke reactive action when a portion of what is left of these beautiful beaches – a portion of the Gulf State Park – is offered for lease to a private developer for operating a hotel and convention center. Knowing full well that any problem of significance will not be solved reactively, I turned to reflection. My reflections took me back to the story of the grassroots work in Kennett Square, PA. The Kennett Square community began their process when a community home health nurse was concerned that they were not solving the teen pregnancy problem. Perhaps every true change in culture or civilization – every true elevation in ethics – is begun when someone feels strongly in their heart that we have a significant problem not being solved in the way we are currently going about things. To begin, problems are never solved elementally – as one well knows through reflection on hygienist work. Filling a cavity never solves the whole problem – one's whole life style is involved in stopping cavities permanently and creating a healthy mouth. So to deal with teen pregnancy, this community leader found the need and way to work on and from the smallest whole that could truly solve it - the community. Through reflection, she saw teen pregnancy cannot be solved one-by-one; the community must change to become a place for healthy teen development and growth; only then will teen pregnancy (and for that matter, teen crime, drug use, etc.) decline, and teen development flourish.

We can look at the current Gulf State Park dilemma in much the same way. What is the smallest whole that we need to hold in mind if we are ever going to do the good and right as far as the beaches are concerned? That smallest whole at least encompasses the ecosystem of these shores and inland waters. As long as we the people remain human centered rather than life of the whole centered in our thinking, there will be no wholistic solutions to the problems caused by our development of this area. Not unlike the work of Kennett Square, which began with reflection on the purpose of teening in relation to community, it seems we would need to begin with reflection on the purpose of beaches as they relate to the estuarial watershed as a whole. And just as they reflected on the virtue of the land of Kennett so that they could take on and harmonize with that virtue as their practical living philosophy, we would have the necessary work of reflecting on the virtue of this land... so that we could harmonize with its virtue in our every act (that is, take our land's virtue as our practical living philosophy).

My own beginnings at this reflective work have led me to see its virtue as being *peaceful, vitalizing and replenishing of our life and all life.* When we go to the beach and truly let its ebb and flow enter us and reorganize our energies, we find our lives become revitalized and replenished... and a sense of peacefulness washes over us. Interestingly, the virtue of a land – when we get it right – is true for all of life, not just human life. Are not the lives of herons, pelicans, osprey, hummingbirds, finches, butterflies, buntings, trout, redfish, dolphins, etc., also vitalized and replenished by the energy field of this area? We could go on and on with examples of the beautiful integrated working of the whole. Yet, we call the Gulf Shores area "Pleasure Island." We drive our processes beginning from economics and pleasure rather than *peace, vitality and replenishment for each and all.*

Change of the sort being imaged requires an entirely different nature of process than "fighting city hall" or "fighting developers." Change of this sort requires a grassroots shift in ethics. We need to become ethical as far as this land we the people are a part of and have responsibility for... and becoming ethical requires we consciously and conscientiously take on and live from a new philosophy - a living philosophy that will rightly guide our ways of living and working. To build a new philosophy requires a new perspective – a perspective whole enough and encompassing enough to promise the nature of ethics we now need to "solve our problems permanently" in a way that is right for each and good for all... to build a new philosophy requires reflecting on the working of the land until we see the essential virtue imbedded in its design.

Reflecting on the story of Kennett Square, one can readily see this is not overwhelming, but truly doable. It can become a work of the heart since our paths are created through reflection and dialogue, the work is inspiriting and the outcomes are vitalizing... and, at the end of the day, we can say, our lives have had purpose and meaning... we made a difference that matters.

After Hurricane Katrina, Need for Reflection

Reflection on images and experiences entering our hearts after Hurricane Katrina tells us of the many who opened themselves to the virtue of *compassion*. Actions of people across the globe made visible and helped us experience the inspirited and inspiriting aspects of being fully and truly human. We are awakened to our potential as human beings: Our potential to overcome life's difficulties, to live in healthy relationship with one another, to help one another to the point of putting our own lives at risk even for the care of "strangers," and our potential for becoming instruments of the Creator's love such that *compassion* might flow through and among all human beings. We are awakened to the truth and the gift that we are so created that spirit can enter us and flow through us as we answer our own unique calling and take on our work and role as living members of the family of life on this earth.

Reflection on the disaster across the Gulf Coast awakens (or reawakens) us to several essential truths, the first being that we are not the source. We – humanity – are neither the center of, nor do we or should we ever have control over, the essential life processes of earth. There is a Source – an Ultimate Source of creation – and we are not it. Second, each and all are members of the living whole of life on earth. As such, if we touch one member of life, we touch all of life. Third, the human being was and is designed with dignity and intended to have dignity. In truth, in essence and in dignity, we are all equal; no one person is above another. Fourth, and most importantly, if love is not in our processes, love will not be in the outcomes.

When we hold in mind all of what we have seen and experienced since the storm, Katrina, and simultaneously hold in our hearts these essential truths, what begins to emerge is the realization we are in a process of moving to a new platform – a new starting point. One way we might say this is that we cannot use the same mind to solve our problems as the mind that created them in the first place. What becomes essential is leading from wholeness and an image of its virtuous working. Movement to this new platform is and will be a grassroots process, for in the face of issues of magnitude, intuition informed by wisdom is what is called for, and we know that both intuition and wisdom come only through quiet minds and open hearts. The perspectives of economics, rights, ownership, law, power, science or even righting wrongs are not whole enough to lead us as a people to a new level of planetary ethics for life and living. Coming to the fore is the need for processes inspired by wisdom, "seen" by intuition, and led by virtue – all of which are possible only if we open our hearts to love, our minds to reflection, and our eyes to potential. By so doing, we may become vessels of the Source for "seeing" and doing what is right for the essence of each, while being good for the whole of all of life.

Leading from virtue, with love in our processes, and guided by a true living philosophy, we have hope of "seeing" what could be for the healthy inspirited healing and living of each and all… we have hope of harmonizing with the virtue of the land... the *soul healing spirit lifting rhythmic flowing* virtue of the Mississippi River watershed.

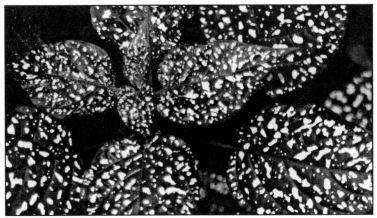

Seven-Generation Affordable Housing

*Essential Work
Towards Creating
Truly American Villages*

There is a growing reality for an ever increasing number of America's people: The elusiveness, the diminishing possibility of affordable housing. What perhaps was the dilemma of those with low incomes is now being shared

by more and more of our citizens, young and old alike. Many of our young people who have done as you are "supposed" to do in America (that is, get a good education, secure a good job, contribute to the well being of society) are discovering that the affordable housing, home ownership element of the American Dream is becoming unreachable – regardless of their work effort and frugality. In the absence of significant financial support from outside their means, home ownership is becoming more and more unlikely. In reality, the "low income" restraint to affordable housing is encompassing larger and larger segments of our population. The escalation in housing costs may very well overtake and consume any advances we have made in securing and establishing affordable housing – even within the current scope of our efforts.

This growing unreachableness certainly seems to be widespread, but perhaps it is most visible within and around the population centers of our country. There is a particular vitality – an aliveness – that is present or potentially present within the neighborhoods, communities, and centrally shared spaces of our cities and their surrounds... a vitality that many are drawn towards – either to move into, or stay – often in trying circumstances. This aliveness is in various states of health. Renovation efforts aimed at physically revitalizing neighborhoods commonly result in affordability diminishing – both for the current residents, and those who would wish to move in. This pattern is repeated time and time again.

At first glance we easily see one possible inevitability. As housing prices become truly unreachable, prices (perhaps very quickly) could collapse. Achieving low prices this way seems fraught with hazard - large numbers of people losing their investments and a housing industry collapsing does not seem to bode well for the health and well being of our society. This is especially true when we consider the systemic nature – touch one element, you touch them all – of our society. How then might we generate *affordability* for each and all of America's people in a stabilizing transitioning sort of way?

Reflecting from the perspective of potential (versus problem) we naturally would be seeking a more wholistic image of affordability... and in so doing, a host of considerations (including but beyond economics) come to the fore. Besides affordable financing, we see the necessity of being affordable from the perspectives of energy source and use, environmental considerations, wise and lasting use of earth's resources, sustainability, and of course life itself. In regards to life, can we afford to live or perhaps even sustain life without spaces and places that are vitalizing and energizing? Is not life – if we are really living – something beyond sustaining material existence and comfort? Is not there a critical aspect of life related to being – beyond stuff and material – an experience of being fully alive, and of participating in the processes of life, its agonies and ecstasies... of sharing and supporting with others... of experiencing joy, sorrow, love, and compassion? Are not these essential processes for sustaining and developing our humanness?

And so we can see much is at stake here, not just a physical house, but a vibrant, spirited, American way of life as well... and we can see that as we work to bring about *affordability*, we must be conscious of and conscientious about the larger whole within which these housing structures are to be generated.

An image of the larger whole that emerges from reflection is that of a village - the vitality, the viability, the life energies and spirit present in a harmoniously working village, a village that is alive with neighborhood, community, education, entertainment, worship, shopping, etc., villages that would spring up within our cities and towns - our centers of population. Each would have their own character – character determined by a common bond and pursuits essential to life. They would share a common wisdom and a common ethic, and would live harmoniously with the planetary energy field within which they resided.

In regards to the financing element of *affordability*, stated most simply, housing (new and renovated) would be constructed against the criteria of *affordability* (energy, environment, etc.), and built to last at least 200 years. Seven-generation structures call for imaging seven-generation financing and seven-generation investing. Yes, with a bit more faith and creativity, housing could be reachable for all.

Since our intent is to create truly American villages, it would seem to be wise that we hold within these, truths of what in a real sense America is about - a place for life, liberty and the pursuit of dignity.

> Life - Experiencing the fullness and wholeness of life.
> Liberty - The freedom to choose the process by which I develop my soul, realize my potential, surrender to my instrumentality, and manifest spirit.
> Dignity - Become fully and truly human in the dignified image intended.

As this reflective process is coming to a close, one more image is emerging, an image that is sourced in a notion held for a long time. In the inspiring dream of Dr. Martin Luther King Jr., he speaks of all gathering around the same table. Such a table does not yet exist, but rather requires us to come together to create it. As we reflect on what has been written, the "table" is beginning to take on the form of "a village."

Awakening the Spirit and Potential of the Upper Peninsula

The Upper Peninsula (the U. P.) of Michigan is the place of my birth – a rugged land of minerals, timber, Great Lakes shores and cold snowy winters... a land I love for its capacity to build character while it awakens you to the beauty and demands of nature. Recently, I was called upon to reflect on this land from a repotentializing perspective – with the hope of creating a charcoal sketch of the potential of the U.P. that will provide a basis for further development.

If efforts we undertake are to be repotentializing in nature – as opposed to improveing what is – we must begin our thinking from the "perspective of potential" versus the "perspective of problem." In regards to the repotentialization of the Upper Peninsula, we would begin by anchoring to and indexing from the virtue of the land itself. Potential is always realized by working out from or being sourced in the essence or core virtue of that which we are trying to realize the potential of. And so we would first have to get a working image – supported by a verbal expression – of the essence or core virtue of the U. P. Now there is an expression (trademarked, I believe) that, to me at least, would be a good starting point – a place from which to begin reflection and dialogue - that statement (from my memory) being, *The Upper Peninsula: Rugged as its coastline, tough as its winters, independent as its people.* ...remembering, of course, that virtue/essence is more of the nature of truth – in that we are not seeking an absolute, but rather a working statement that through time will unfold and deepen in meaning.

Working from the virtue of the land, we could develop a living philosophy – a "Yooper" way of living and working – out from which would emerge, develop and evolve value adding processes - value adding processes that would not only reflect the essential character of the U.P., but would also provide the organizing point for doing business and for businesses. Doing this would certainly make possible – move us closer towards making real – a business teacher's statement to his students, "You don't have to leave the U. P. to be successful in business," a statement that I perceive as not only a belief, but a dream – a dream of the character and nature expressed by Dr. Martin Luther King Jr., which is important to remember because for those who would take on a leadership role – the role of leading from virtue – there will be the requirement to draw forth spirit and energy accessible only through true dream and vision.

Continuing, here are some thoughts on essential value adding processes:

- Tourism. From the perspective of harmonizing with the virtue of the land, tourism would develop, not as the "entertaining type," but as the skill, and self-reliance development made available through the energy field of the U. P.
- Metals/Metallurgy. Regardless of the ornateness of the artifact or product, it would have "inbuilt" the toughness and capacity to sustain its performance – ongoingly - without complaint. None of the metals – be they castle hinges and doors, or space age material - would easily or readily give way to fatigue.
- Woods/woodworking. It is a strength and an essential requirement for maintaining the spirit of "Yoopers" to see the beauty in all… regardless of the tough or challenging work that may follow. Witness how often you hear or find yourself saying, "Isn't that beautiful," in regards to a snowfall… knowing full well it may take a day or more to "dig out." As I have reflected on "Yooper" value adding processes, the image of the natural (essence) beauty of the wood, regardless of the ruggedness of the work for which it was designed, would always be visible and present.
- Education. Regardless of subject matter, education would have a character building component – a component that acknowledges "independence" which perhaps transcends itself to "manifesting unique-

ness," but in either case never loses sight of "we're in this together" (for example, in a snowstorm), and thus the necessity for working together, helping each other… a component that develops the capacity for "plain speaking" – for straight forward interaction.

A few thoughts about schooling, and the development of our children and resources form the last piece of the charcoal sketch. I recall an experience I had when consulting with a company that produced turbines for jet engines, and the interaction with an accomplished metal sculptor who I met through some community development work. What I discovered was the technological understanding required to produce the castings for large sculptures was of similar depth to that required for casting jet engine turbines. The point here is that the nature of value adding processes will require an evolving depth of craftsmanship – of the nature and tradition of craftsmen who develop and advance the technology of their work. The institutions that would be called upon to play a role in these processes would need to advance metal and wood technology beyond that which is currently understood. Tourism and education would require similar advances in understanding and process delivery.

Well, that is the charcoal sketch. There is no question that the sketch covers a bit of territory – hopefully enough territory to build an image of sufficient wholeness that we gain a "taste" of its doability. As I looked over the sketch, I experienced a real sense of hope and possibility – hope because the virtue of the U. P. is still accessible (it has not been artificially obscured), and hope from the knowledge that there is still present sufficient "U. P. character" that could be awakened and out from which could emerge leaders and leadership - people who would respond to and lead from virtue, those who would see it, and experience it as a true calling.

Taking a Stance for Ethics

Ethics, true ethics, when they are really working, are completely and totally free of the motivations of fear, punishment and reward. Ethics are merely the expression and manifestation of the right

71

and good. In this way – in the presence of will – we can be truly authentic in the stands we take or the stances we hold toward the seeing and carrying out of the right and good. Fortunately the capacity to see and live out the right and good is inherent in our design, and is both accessible and developable through conscious and conscientious effort.

In a similar way, ethics, when they are truly working within our organizations, are equally free of mindsets such as efficiency and economics. Having the dedicated discipline to "hold a stance" until the ethics – the right and good – relative to the situation is clearly seen and understood is essential to being ethical. Once the right and good is clear, then such things as efficiency and economics can enter as essential or critical parameters (versus "mindsets") that demand attention and effort as the work is carried out. It is in some ways an act of faith to accept and be confident in the notion that the mind that can clearly see and understand the right and good will readily and creatively see ways to achieve the required economics and efficiencies.

This act of faith, however, is somewhat bolstered by experience. Every master carpenter understands that if we maintain our focus on a particular effect – *squareness* for example – efficiencies and economies of construction will follow. Efficiencies and economies seem to be the "gift" of taking a stance towards *squareness.* At the same time, master carpenter experience shows that when efficiency and economics dominate (become mindsets rather than parameters), *squareness* quickly drops off – often eventually disappearing.

Continuing our contemplation – in what may seem to be a leap of faith to some, but regardless is the emerging image – we can begin to see a possible start point for organiza-

tions that take on the aim of becoming and being ethical. By having clearly defined standards specific to our work and guiding principles emerging from clarity of our purpose, we can begin to establish a context for ethics. From purpose and principles can emerge the capacity to fill and live out roles – the role of the organization in regards to the larger whole of which it is a part and which it serves, as well as individual roles within the organization. Taken together – clarity around what our work is, the required standards, and our way of working as established by our purpose and principles – we may indeed have a reasonable start point…
a start point, certainly not an end point, for taking on and developing the character and characteristic of being ethical.

Respiritualizing Culture

At a recent community dinner in the high desert of Utah, a subject matter that came up was in regards to the Navajo people, and the dilemma that exists relative to their desire to preserve their culture and the necessity to generate favorable economics. It is this subject matter that is the source of these continued reflections… reflections that started shortly after that interaction. While this reflection process is ongoing, some of what has emerged is being shared here, with the hope that these thoughts are sufficiently complete and whole as to provide reflective material as we continue to reflect on the culture and economic dilemma.

Culture is a process, a life process, an essential life process. It is the way of the people – the people's way of living, way of working, way of worshipping, honoring, dignifying, celebrating, etc. Culture, when it is truly working, is in reality a living being. As such it experiences all that is true for life. It struggles to sustain itself, to develop, to evolve, and strives to become. Like all of life, it is intended and so designed to have purposes - purposes that relate to service and work in regards to the larger wholes of which it is a part – in particular the whole of life. These purposes, when authentic, are the means by which spirit enters into our processes. It is the taking on and fulfilling of these purposes that sustains the vitality and viability of the living being we call culture. As purpose diminishes – begins to fade from our consciousness – vitality and viability also diminish… and our ableness to access spirit degrades as well.

These reflections remind me of a golden eagle I once knew. There is a place, a wildlife preserve - dedicated to geese - that I visited annually during the migration season, particularly the fall migration. For some reason, never understood by myself, there lived at this place a golden eagle in a supersized bird cage. In the dozen or so years that I visited this place, I would always stop and spend a few moments observing this eagle. I especially found the eye contact to be quite powerful in ways that I could not, nor did I seek to, describe. Over the years there took place a definite and distinctive downward shift in the state and demeanor of this eagle – a decline that was particularly noticeable in the expression of its eyes. Eyes that were once filled with light and spirit grew dimmer and dimmer though time. I began to sense his eagleness was disappearing. Yes he was genetically, biologically and scientifically a reasonably healthy full fledged eagle... but to me, and seemingly to the eagle as well, his eagleness was disappearing.

Given these images and the understanding of the living nature of culture with the accompanying requirement for active carrying out of purpose in order to access spirit, sustain vitality and viability, preservation seems to me at least to be a not so useful term or notion relative to one's culture. Preservation tends to conjure up images of protection, protective cages, protection from outside influences, etc. Yet, culture is the people's way of contributing to the betterment of life... the life of all, of life itself. Right and good interactions and reciprocal maintenance are essential to one's culture as well as to the whole of life; without such, one can neither maintain health nor sustain existence. Thus enclosing one's culture - seeking to be a closed system versus a living system - would seem to be a very hazardous through time approach – hazardous to the people, hazardous to life, perhaps understandable and justifiable for a bit of time, but not a viable or hope-filled long term strategy. A term or notion that lifts up hope and more useful images is "respiritualization."

Now culture, authentic culture, that is, "the intended ways of being and doing" versus "how things are done," has as its source, virtue, spirit and truth. The values we commonly associate with cultures, if they are authentic and real, are always sourced in, imbued with, and colored by virtue, spirit and truth. Values are manifestations of particular virtues. Culture works to gain access to spirit as well as to be a means for manifesting spirit... that spirit that we gain access to only through the taking on of purposes – purposes in service of larger wholes. Also, cultures are authentic to the degree they are in harmony with essential truths. Reflecting further we notice a significant difference between a cultural value that is in tune with, and acknowledging of, its source versus one that is "disconnected," if you will, from its source. Take freedom as an example. Disconnected from its source, one might think of or experience freedom as "doing your own thing," "doing as you please," "without regard for..." If we reflect on the value freedom imbued with the virtue dignity, we can readily see and experience a difference, a higher order difference... and if we carry our example further to include the perspective of potential, we can begin to see freedom as the liberty to choose the process by which I develop my soul, realize my potential, and surrender to my instrumentality. Out from this we can see the hazard in pursuing values disconnected from their life sources – hazard not only to self, but to the whole of life. Conversely we can see the hope and promise within connected values.

In regards to economics, our reflection turns away from the perspective of problem (a problem to solve) towards the perspective of potential (a potential to be realized). The perspective of potential does not begin with existence, but rather seeks to see and understand essence and then works to create processes where essence is manifested – made real and tangible – into existence. The aim would be to create processes that not only provide a means for generating economics, but ones that would also enable the respiritualization of the Navajo culture... processes that through reflection and dialogue call upon the creative energy, creativity and spirit of the Navajo people. Such an aim lifts up the hope that the wisdom, virtue, spirit and understanding of the Navajo could be put to work in service of the larger wholes of which they are a part – the whole of humanity, the whole of life, mother earth, and her life giving processes.

Reflecting on what has been written, particularly in the previous paragraph, one can readily see boundaries that would need to be crossed – both for the Navajo and for all of earth's people. But then realizing potential – advancing our selves along the path of becoming more fully and truly human, fulfilling the intent and design of the Creator – has, and seemingly always will, require and demand of us boundary crossing, both inwardly and outwardly. We also notice the demand for faith – a faith, bolstered however, by experience... faith in the intent and design of the Creator... faith that right and good outcomes will emerge from conscientious and conscious effort to fulfill this intent... and faith that with clarity and integrity of purpose, that which is needed will be provided; it will show up in one way or another.

A final thought appears in our reflective process, this thought being in regards to the history – the struggles and travails – of the Navajo people: There is a nature of contriteness that is borne out of fear and/or guilt. There is however another nature of contriteness borne out of love and sorrow – true sorrow for potential that is being stymied – and in danger of being lost. It is the latter that will be present in working from the perspective of potential.

Respiritualization requires reflection, dialogue and true intuition – processes of great familiarity to the Navajo people. Herein lies the hope.

Essence lights up
Who We Are

If we take our identity from a class or classification –red, white, black, or yellow, woman, man, gay, straight, young, old, religious, non-religious, and on

and on – we find we are often limiting our cause or purpose to a struggle to gain and access rights. We turn to legality as a means of achieving and sustaining these rights. At the same time, we are running the risk of others seeing us as a member of a category, blind to our uniqueness and our essence. We too run the risk of beginning our thoughts of our self with that which colors our essence (for example, our femaleness, maleness, blackness, whiteness, etc.) rather than that which reflects our true self.

If we anchor our thoughts – our reflective thoughts – in essence and potential, and if we seek and discover ways to manifest that essence in our work and the roles we take on within our community, it becomes possible for us to realize our potential: To fulfill the intent and design of our Creator, both as an individual, and as a living system or socio-eco community. This is the way of dignity – of understanding and realizing the dignity of each and all. From this we can determine an appropriate pattern of rights, a pattern that enables the realization of the open-ended potential of each and all, a pattern that opens us up to our essential potential. People, striving to truly operate from and exist in potential, travel a path that illuminates uniqueness and essence and transcends all sense of hierarchical classes and classifications.

Seeing Essential Virtue and Discovering Essential Role

The other day, while driving home, I caught on the radio a few minutes of an interview with some women of Kenya who are involved in "The Greenbelt Movement" started by Wangari Maathai, the 2004 Nobel Peace Prize winner. What a wonderful and hopeful story it was. To listen as they described the intuitive grasping of the ecological essence of Kenya and the initiation and sustaining of a grassroots movement was, for me, an exciting and moving experience. The vision Wangari Maathai generated as she reflected upon what she saw and experienced as she went about her veterinary work (with malnourished cattle, infected with brown ticks) was a beautiful example of intuition, in that she "saw" the whole of her land, its essence, its right and good working, and within that, a critical process – reforestation, with the real work of planting trees - that needed to be carried out in regards to revitalizing the ecological essence and sociological health of Kenya. Not only did she "see," but she found within and through her heart the courage and conviction to lead from the virtue of compassion – the essence of our humanness – and from the virtue of her land, its ecological essence.

Joan Holliday, of Kennett Square, PA, along with her community, is also striving to lead from virtue - the intuitively knowable, experientially verifiable essence - of her land, this virtue being seen and understood as the intended working of the land... or in the language of Joan and members of her community, "living philosophy of the land." At the heart of their work is the perspective and philosophy of potential, a living philosophy that anchors itself in essence, and fully acknowledges the life nature of human beings – the reality of our being people of earth and members in the community of life... a living philosophy that, like the women of Kenya, brings with it much hope... hope because as we reflect upon our current reality – the current world situation – we, with increasing clarity and conviction, see a void – an absence of and necessity for planetary ethics... yes, planetary ethics – ethical principles of behavior for the whole of earth – for humanity, for all of life.

The work of generating ethics has been and is that of philosophy - a way of discipline - from which can emerge and emanate ethics. Now planetary ethics, if they are to be truly planetary, need to deal with and in a real way enable us to reconcile and transcend the troublesome issues of today… issues such as race, religion, environment, etc. Planetary ethics would similarly acknowledge our "one worldness," the reality of each and all being connected, and the truth of our design: We, as living human beings, are members in the community of life, and as such are equally dependent - co-dependent with our fellow life members - on the vitality and viability of mother earth and her life giving, life generating processes.

Generating planetary ethics requires a "source philosophy" that has sufficient depth, wholeness and inclusivity to embrace that which true planetary ethics needs to encompass. The perspective and living philosophy of potential seems to be a viable candidate - an anchor point, a starting place for such a journey.

Besides what is expressed so far, there are, as we look about our world, other positive spirit-lifting signs. Yes, beyond the reactivity and negative energy are some genuine, evolutionary in nature, stirrings… stirrings like signs of spring from a long and cold winter… stirrings that are struggling to give rise to an evolutionary shift, that is, an unfolding to a higher order platform upon which to live and work. We see a growing interest in a purpose driven life - purpose that brings up and recognizes the need for philosophy - philosophy, not merely as a subject of study, but rather that from which to live in a disciplined way.

The notion of intelligent design is also another hopeful stirring, an indicator of our aliveness, our ability to resist ultimate mechanicalness. It represents a response, perhaps an instinctive life response, to the obvious hazard to humanity should reality be solely defined by and reduced to the physical, the factual, the material, the provable, with the accompanying likelihood of our believing or acting as if we are the source. We know, if not in our minds, certainly in our hearts, that much of life – much of its realness – lies beyond the plane of the physical. At the same time we can see and observe the physical likenesses, the seemingly related progressions, and increasing complexity of life forms presented by life science and the theory of evolution, and with a bit of effort we can understand some of the mechanisms described – all of which emanate from the gift of reason – and which seem to me at least to be quite reasonable when you restrict your perspective to the physical plane of existence… the common platform for scientific endeavors out of which has emerged a knowledge base that we have come to depend on, to rely upon, for much of our daily existence. However, in addition to reason, we human beings have a capacity to access wisdom. Intuitively we know it is not wise to reduce life to the material, for to do so, at the very least, diminishes and in a real way could lead to our dismissing the being and will aspects of ourselves – our very centers for meaning and purpose in our lives. In a similar way we would know it is not wise to throw away a knowledge base that we need and use in so many aspects of our daily existence.

There is much hope in the current arguments between the theories of evolution and intelligent design. Again from my perspective, I believe that as wisdom begins to penetrate, these arguments (arguing that seems at times to have the character of being tainted by power, power over), will shift to discussions and dialogues about role… about the role, work and purpose of scientific endeavor, of religion, of other human processes. Eventually we will have a much better understanding of this living system we call human society; we will "see" the whole of it and the right and good working of its systemic elements – the critical roles and the seemingly huge, somewhat impossible task of generating planetary ethics will come within reach of our grasp. Leading from virtue and virtuous leaders are and will emerge; guided by our conscience and the work of our heart, we – one tree at a time – will move along the path of our becoming... becoming that which we are intended to be: Fully and truly human. It is within us, already present... a potential to be realized. Therein lies the hope. My, what an exciting time to be alive.

Awakening America to a New Mission

The ethical regeneration of automobiling through the awakening of the creative genius, indomitable spirit, and inherent goodness of America and her people.

Many decades ago America brought into this world a totally new structure and process – the automobile and automobiling. A wondrous invention it was… and is. And through making it available to the masses – rather than limiting it to a select few – America and her people experienced a freedom hitherto unknown… a *freedom of access*; a freedom to seek out and be at one with others; freedom to explore, to grow and develop through real experiences, to move about, to seek out and develop opportunities, and to pursue one's potential.

If today we pause and reflect on the current reality of auto-mobiling, we see its essential virtue of *freedom of access* is significantly obscured and severely challenged. No matter where our eyes fall upon the tapestry of automobiling, we see difficult issues and problems… issues and problems that for a growing number of Americans (and beyond) have become a source of concern, worry, angst and increasing divisiveness - issues such as employment, gridlock, America's leadership position, health and safety, environ-ment, community viability, etc. These issues have tended to be considered from a problem solving or financial perspec-tive – neither of which, by nature, has the solving power required. What does show up for us, through reflection and dialogue (versus analysis and argument) is the necessity for a new platform from which to operate – a new perspective. Now in order to shift platforms – to move up – we need to consider and see potential - to develop capacity to hold the perspective of potential; and we need to lead from virtue – the essence of that which we are trying to advance or real-ize the potential of.

Holding the perspective of potential, we contemplate ethics and ethical behavior. It is both natural and right that we begin to question ourselves as to what is our obligation – both to humankind and to the life processes of earth –

opposite the current reality, the real condition of automobiling, and the automobile itself. If we add to our consideration the pending explosion of automobiling in China, as its immense population begins to embrace *freedom of access* which has been commonly held in America, we notice a real sense of urgency bubbling up within ourselves... an urgency to not only transcend the multitude of issues and problems facing American automobiling, but also to lead development of a new structure and process, one which would provide for the global community and mother earth a more virtuous, a more right and good relationship with the automobile and automobiling. Accepting that we cannot solve a problem at the level at which it was created, that the nature of work required at this time is not improvement, but rather regenerative – a respiriting, ethical repotentializing - and that we Americans have the obligation and, thankfully, the creative inventiveness, indomitable spirit, and inherent goodness needed to lead the world in the development of this next platform... accepting this, we can proceed to lift ourselves up, to come together, and get on with this critical work.

Now if we are to proceed, the processes we use must call upon and bring forth will and spirit (the common tools of motivation and energy are inadequate for repotentializing). We are at a critical time for America and her people – a telling time indeed. At such times in the past, leadership has emerged that not only provides a vision through which spirit and will can be accessed, but also the particular: An operationable component of the larger vision. Kennedy's call to put a man on the moon was such a particular. Specific to automobiling, given its current state, *"injury free, nonpolluting automobiling."* would be analogous to Kennedy's man on the moon. As we reflect on, dialogue and develop this notion, we can see it would truly be a step change – a new, higher order, ethical platform - a notion that genuinely has the potential to ethically regenerate – to repotentialize automobiling and the automobiling industry… a vision and mission that naturally would call upon and demand the best and the true character of America and her people. Can you not just see the creativity, the excitement, the sense of hope and goodness that would emerge as we came together as people, as companies, as communities, as citizens of the world?

This is not an unreal or "pie in the sky" quest. Much of the required technology has or is being developed, especially true if we look beyond the auto industry. New integrations will be required. Coalescing decisions will need to be made (power systems, for example) so that resources can be focused and effectively managed. Wise government encour-

agement and influence will be required… and certainly this pursuit is not beyond the developable capacity and inner characteristics of America's people. The opportunity to regain freedom, to truly feel good about ourselves, to demonstrate our potential and spirit… and the truth that we really do care about our fellow citizens and earth itself, are powerful forces that will work to enable and inspirit this mission.

A Negentropic
Vision of Automobiling

Regarding the inevitable and necessary direction of the automobiling industry, the concepts of sustainability and competing come up in the form of questions. The purpose of this writing is to share a few thoughts in regards to these concepts – thoughts that could be explored further.

It is important to understand that sustainability can only be achieved by active and appropriate ethics being integrated into that which has an upward thrust. In other words, ethics, ethical behavior, will by necessity be the way of working for those who will be participating in the process of sustainability. Also, trying to achieve sustainability by focusing only on arresting entropy (run down) or by trying to be neutral (non-harmful) is inadequate. Negentropic (run up) work is necessary. In the case of automobiling (and true for many others), we can see a path – *nonpolluting, injury free automobiling* – that not only has an upward thrust, but effectively arrests entropy as well. Given this reality, it becomes quite obvious that we need both an understanding of ethics – what is appropriate and sufficiently encompassing – and a clear mission/operationable vision such that an upward thrust can be pursued. With these we can have both the firm ground to stand upon and an ethical base for competition and competing – competing in ways that will produce a better world for our own children and for all children.

As I reflected on the concept of competing, I recalled a conversation I had with a business leader from Canon. We were discussing development, realizing one's potential and the uniqueness of each and all – a natural subject given that development is a common process in Japanese philosophy. He offered the thought that if we focused on developing our uniqueness there would be sufficient space for each and all to compete – implying of course there is no need (or wisdom for that matter) in each and all of us trying to occupy the same space. I also reflected upon competition as the Greeks viewed it. They tended to see it as a means to excel together; they discovered that if one person ran against another, both ran faster. So the aim of competition was not so much the victory (or "killing the competition") as it was a means to get better and better, not only as individuals within an industry, but as an industry itself. The American version of this shows up in county fairs and trade fairs. Here we hold competitions of demonstrated capability with clear recognition by knowledgeable people as to whose skill or product is the best. Transparency is often present such that the skill is demonstrated in a way that all could see – the only question being did those who were observing have the willfulness and dedication to develop the required ableness? Here the competition – its aim – is all about advancing one's own ableness, the ableness of the trade and the industry. The focus is not upon the nature of victory and defeat that engenders hatred, for nothing is more effective at diminishing ethics (thus sustainability) than hatred... the same hatred that diminishes our capacity to advance our humanness. Fairness, cooperation and competition are essential values of the American way of life, and will certainly be called into play in the step change being demanded of the automobiling industry.

Moving to this new platform will require a few shifts in our perspective. We will have to anchor and encompass our thinking in virtue and wholeness (for example, the virtue of automobiling, the virtues of America and her people, the wholeness of an industry, the wholeness of the planet earth). These will provide the anchors, the context, the mission, and operationable vision for our pursuit of sustainability.

Hopefully this "charcoal sketch" is sufficient to give a sense of the nature of thinking and work called for in the automobiling industry and for realizing sustainability. In closing, we are reminded of a comment by Einstein:

"We shall require a substantially new manner of thinking if mankind is to survive."

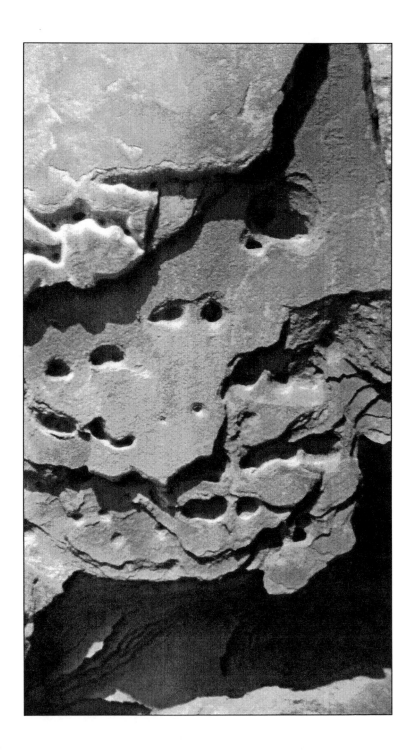

The Working of the Black Canyon of the Gunnison

While visiting the Black Canyon of the Gunnison in Colorado, it is quite common to have a feeling - an intuitive sense - that the way the Black Canyon speaks to us is unique. There is something about the way the Black Canyon works on us when we are reflectively present that has importance and significance to us as a people. The Black Canyon opens us up, not in a gentle way, but more in a forceful, direct, but caring way. It not only enables us to see and experience our connectedness with earth, but

causes within us an ongoing reflection about earth – her working – and about who we are as a people – where we come from, why we are here, where we are headed. Perhaps it was this experience that caused Reverend Mark Warner to so zealously pursue its preservation. It was this sense of the way the Black Canyon works that brought to the fore the image of the question, "Who will speak for earth?" being visibly present at the Black Canyon. It is the nature of question, the nature of reflection, that would naturally occur – have its origin - at the Black Canyon… for this question, not unlike the Black Canyon itself, puts a very different - out of the ordinary - demand upon us… a much different demand than that required to "speak of earth," the common practice when pursuing the work of arresting entropy.

Reflecting further on having visibly present this question, "Who will speak for earth?" we naturally turn to all those special places that currently "speak of earth," particularly those places that we have set aside or recognize as places where we experience a connectedness to the natural world… places that commonly, often in an organized way, "speak of earth." Regarding that which is uniquely present in these places… such things as the beauty, the flora and fauna, the history, the geological nature and processes, the particular life processes occurring and being served in these, and the unique way a particular place speaks to us, it seems truly natural and very appropriate that in addition to "speaking of earth," these set-aside places could serve as reflective spaces for the added question, "Who will speak for earth?"… and by so doing, enable us to see and experience the magic of one place in a way that allows us to better connect to and see the whole, the life of the whole, and the whole of life on earth… thereby providing real means for us to have access to the spirit and truth required to develop the planetary ethics so urgently needed.

Essence of our Developmental Work as Young Adults

The capacity to develop a real and relevant living philosophy is critical to sustaining the upward thrust of the intended unfolding of life on earth.

As we human beings reach the developmental phase of life we call young adulthood, it becomes necessary for us

to build for ourselves, and in common with our peers, a frame of reference from which to live our lives. This frame of reference is necessarily different from the one our parents and elder guides have provided, different not just because we want it to be our own (although of course, there is a bit of that feeling of power – or energization – one experiences from stepping beyond the boundaries), but different because the world in which we now live has changed. How best can we develop a frame of reference to carry us on our life path? To start with, our frame of reference must be whole enough and encompassing enough to answer the larger questions about life and living before us – questions such as what is the meaning of life? What is my work and role within life? Why is there conflict and suffering, etc? This frame of reference must be large enough to include the greater experiences of this world, and give hope of coming together as a people to resolve issues facing us and the earth today. It should acknowledge and make ever more real the unique role and work for which we were designed and to which we are being called. In the absence of a frame of reference whole enough and complete enough to include the reality of the world before us, we will be unprepared to take on our life responsibilities.

To become whole as a person calls for both faith and philosophy; or perhaps more clearly, both faith and wisdom (recall that the meaning of philosophy is love of wisdom). The world today – our world - is starving for philosophy, philosophy that gives meaning to life, encompasses our being as well as our function, while interconnecting the whole of life on earth such that it will become possible for people of all faiths – faiths that believe in one Source of creation, people who have at heart the well being of humanity - to come together in dialogue… dialogue that will lead to creating planetary ethics that address the critical planetary issues of this day - hunger, ecology and harmonious cohabitation of earth, to name but a few.

And so, essential and critical is to begin our work of creating a living philosophy that has within it the essence of the truth of love... one that includes not only human function, but more essentially human being... one that encompasses the whole of humanity while embracing the dignity of each... one that acknowledges our membership and part within the life of the whole and the whole of life on this earth... and one that sees we human beings are not outside of life, but designed and created to be a part of life, and therefore each have a role in its work and working. Intuitively, we know the need for living philosophy. We know and experience the world we live in and the planetary issues we face in that world. And we know there is a void in our lives; that void being a living philosophy from which to live our lives and face these issues, not as separate individuals, but as community. For ultimately our work in the world must lead us as a people of earth to a healthier, more whole, and more hopeful life. To build such a philosophy requires guiding help – guideposts - along the way. To build such a philosophy calls for reflection and dialogue that enable coming to grips with essential questions. To build a living philosophy takes the mind and heart beyond the world we live in and beyond our own issues to humanity as a whole and all of life on earth.

This developmental process begins in our adult youth, and since it puts us on a path in pursuit of truth, marks the beginning of a lifelong journey... a journey of searching for ultimate truths from which to live our lives and through which we find the way – our own unique way – to return to the Source that which we have been given by the Source.

Reflecting on the Working of Love

Love... continuously emanates from the Essence of creation, its true and only Source. With unfailing alertness and infinite patience, love seeks an opening through

which it can flow... the means by which it can enter into the working of the world. In the absence of an open vessel, a receptive heart, love cannot enter the world... and a love-less world ceases to work, ceases to be, and brings unimaginable suffering to its Creator.

Upon entry, love works not to gain power... nor does it pursue power and authority over others; it seeks not to dominate, nor to be understood. Love seeks to illuminate and gain understanding of.

Love casts not shadows... it is pure light... a light that freely enters a receptive heart - a beckoning instrument. Love, once welcomed, goes about its work of reflecting from and among one another... a reflecting that awakens faith, breathes life into hope, and strengthens spirit. Love illuminates ultimate truths... the truth of our instrumentality... the illusion of our being a source... the truth of our oneness and equality... the reality that but for our Creator, no one is superior. Love celebrates uniqueness as it works to unfold and manifest essence.

While love holds salvation as its purpose... love has as its ultimate aim lighting the path of evolution of our being... the path by which we ultimately become that which was and is intended: A perfect reflection of the image from and through which we were created. Love enters and lights our path in ways that sustain our longing to return and our ever-strengthening yearning to become. Always beckoning and occasionally admonishing us along our intended path of progression, love lightens the burden of our soul... yet calls attention to and provides focus to the work before us.

Love lights the way... and leads us to advance our humanness beyond love based on or restricted to common or shared blood... to embrace one another, each and all members of the human family, as brothers and sisters – neighbors, one and all.

As we, humankind, progress along our path, and our capacity for embracing the working of love deepens, our work becomes increasingly intrinsic... requiring more inner acceptance and a freer and more conscious choice. This is not realizable through external forces (that is., authority or persuasion, reason and logical argument, commands, threats, fear or guilt), but more and more through the work of our heart and the working of our conscience. Each new progression does not diminish the significance of the previous, nor lessen it being required... rather, that which comes before becomes enfolded into the new... with deeper and truer meaning, and a greater possibility of being truly lived out.

Thus the new progression - to embrace the whole of life, to understand and honor its working, and to nourish and bring forth life's potential and its processes - does not diminish the love required and intended between and among our brothers and sisters. Nor does it lessen, but rather makes more real, the truth of our dignity and equality. And, as we as humanity continue our progression along our path, love's working calls upon and requires many more, not fewer, receptive hearts and willful instruments... especially now, with oneness and wholeness being brought to the fore. These receptive hearts become the focal points of the light, of that which is to be understood and served... the aim of our work.

That which love illuminates and wisdom enables us to see, brings to faith a new dimension and added perspective. Faith that has sustained the path of our return and salvation now adds the dimension of our instrumentality and role in the ongoing creation... for humankind was not intended nor designed as the end point of creation, but rather as an instrument with an authentic and genuine co-creator role... a role in the unfolding, and yet to be unfolded majesty and mystery of creation... a role that requires we become fully and truly human... thus fulfilling and perfecting the intent and design of the Creator... and therein lies the hope.

GUIDING PRINCIPLES

Perhaps now is a good time to gather our community (our community of friends, family, colleagues, etc.) together to read aloud, reflect and dialogue.

And as we gather our community, let us discipline ourselves to stay on the path, using these guiding principles:

·Anchor ourselves to the virtue of the land.
·Seek wholistic approaches rather than partial solutions.
·Take all issues to essence.
·Pursue that which vitalizes all.
·Take a role that follows the work of the heart.

…always remembering,

If love is not present in our processes,
Love will not be present in the outcomes.